Singles Skating

BY HEATHER E. SCHWARTZ

Consultant:
Kristin Eberth
United States Figure Skating double gold medalist
Professional figure skater with Disney On Ice

CAPSTONE PRESS
a capstone imprint

Snap Books are published by Capstone Press,
1710 Roe Crest Drive, North Mankato, Minnesota 56003
www.mycapstone.com

NOV 0 1 2017

Library of Congress Cataloging-in-Publication Data
Names: Schwartz, Heather E., author. | Eberth, Kristin, consultant
Title: Singles skating / by Heather Schwartz ; consultant: Kristin Eberth
    USFS Double Gold Medalist Professional Figure Skater with Disney On Ice.
Description: North Mankato, Minnesota : Capstone Press, 2018. | Series: Snap
    Books. Figure Skating | Includes bibliographical references and index. |
    Audience: Age 8–9. | Audience: Grade 4 to 6.
Identifiers: LCCN 2017009727
ISBN 9781515781882 (library binding)
ISBN 9781515781929 (eBook PDF)
Subjects: LCSH: Figure skating—Juvenile literature. | Figure
    skaters—Biography—Juvenile literature.
Classification: LCC GV850.4 .S387 2018 | DDC 796.91/2—dc23
LC record available at https://lccn.loc.gov/2017009727

Editorial Credits
Brenda Haugen, editor; Veronica Scott, designer; Kelli Lageson,
media researcher; Kathy McColley, production specialist

Photo Credits
Newscom: Icon SMI 147/Michael Tureski, cover, Icon SMI/DPPI/Philippe
Millerau, 26, ZUMA Press/Bildbyran, 13 (bottom), ZUMA Press/Peter
KrtGer, 29; Shutterstock: anfisa focusova, 3, bitt24, 23, Dmitry Morgan, 14,
Dmytro Zinkevych, 22, ID1974, 5, 28, Iurii Osadchi, 21, Nicholas Piccillo,
6, Olga Besnard, 11, 12, 15, 16, 18, 19, 25, Paolo Bona, 9, PrinceOfLove, 17,
Rawpixel.com, 24, SergiyN, 7, Shooter Bob Square Lenses, cover, throughout,
testing, 8, 13 (top)

Design elements: Shutterstock

Printed and bound in Canada.
010395F17

Table of Contents

Style, Form, and Grace

A single skater stands in a pose in the center of the rink. The music begins, and she starts to move with it. She times her **choreography** to the rhythm of the music. Her sequined outfit catches the spotlight, bringing a dramatic quality to the program. But the skater is focused on form, not the audience. She aims to showcase the talent she has honed through hard work and practice before the competition.

The crowd gasps as the skater wobbles off balance during a turn. They cheer as she demonstrates an amazing jump with a graceful landing. They glance at the judges, hoping for a good score. The skater has high hopes too. While she skates, however, she thinks only of her next move on the ice.

Fast Fact

Sonia Henie was a famous singles skater in the 1920s and 1930s. She was the first figure skater to use dance choreography in her routines.

At the song's end, the audience applauds. The judges prepare their scores. The skater holds a triumphant ending pose. She may have made mistakes, but she overcame them to finish her program. She knows she did her best.

All skaters who choose singles figure skating have the chance to perfect amazing skills. They perform programs that demonstrate skill, style, and personality.

choreography—the arrangement of steps, movements, and required elements that make up a singles skating routine

Chapter 1

Basics and Rules

When singles figure skaters perform, they seem to glide effortlessly around the ice. Watching them spin, glide, and jump can inspire anyone to try their moves. It's not an easy sport to master. But if you're willing to put in the time and energy, you can learn to move gracefully while performing on the ice too.

The journey starts with learning basic skating skills. Group lessons or private lessons can teach you how to skate forward and backward and make simple turns. From there, you can learn more advanced skills. Eventually you may even want to compete as a singles skater. Then you get to have the fun of skating to music in a glamorous costume.

Practice doesn't require anything but ice and the proper equipment. No fancy clothing is needed. Wear clothing you can move in that also keeps you warm. Remember your gloves or mittens, and always wear a sports helmet to protect against falls. Make sure your figure skates fit comfortably while also offering support.

Skate Fit

When you try on a pair of figure skates, put your heel all the way to the back of the boot. Lace it up, and walk around on the rubber floor matting. Figure skates shouldn't feel tight or uncomfortable. They should not pinch your toes, but they should feel snug. Make sure your foot doesn't slide around in the boot. Your heel shouldn't slip up either.

Lacing can change how your skates feel. Boots should be laced tighter across your foot and around your ankle. They can be a little looser at the top to allow for movement. Cross extra lace length over the hooks, not around the top of your boot. Knot the laces so they don't become untied while you're skating.

FOLLOW THE RULES

When skaters decide to get competitive, they start out at the basic skills level. More advanced levels include intermediate, novice, junior, and senior. Skaters must pass a skills test in order to advance to the next level.

The **International** Skating Union (ISU) sets the rules for skaters in competition. The rules even cover how skaters should dress. Costumes must be athletic and not theatrical. Decorations are allowed, but they must be attached to the costume so they will not fall off on the ice. Male skaters must wear full-length pants. They are not allowed to wear tights.

The rules also cover the skating program. They explain how points are taken away for falls and other interruptions. They outline how programs are scored. Skaters and coaches should be familiar with the rules.

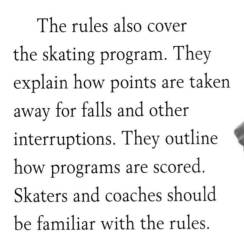

Fast Fact

Before the 1200s, skate blades were made of animal bones.

international—between or among the nations of the world

Chapter 2

Footwork, Jumps, and Spins

Skaters must master many skills. U.S. Figure Skating encourages learning the basics, including footwork, jumps, and spins. That way, skaters will be ready to move on and up and even compete in the sport.

FOOTWORK

Footwork in figure skating is also called a step sequence. It's a set of moves that follow one after the other. These moves include:

Bracket

Skaters turn in a pattern that creates a bracket, or parenthesis, shape on the ice.

Choctaw

Skaters turn by switching feet and changing edges from outside to inside or inside to outside.

Crossover

Skaters gain speed and turn corners by crossing one foot over the other.

Mohawk

Skaters glide on a curve with one foot to turn forward to backward and backward to forward, each edge forming parts of the same curve.

Rocker

Skaters turn on one foot without changing edges.

Twizzle

Skaters turn and rotate on one foot.

inside edge

toe pick

outside edge

JUMPS

Jumps come in many styles and send figure skaters into the air. They include edge jumps and toe jumps. Examples include:

Axel Jump

Skaters launch using the forward outside edge and land on the opposite foot's back outside edge. The Axel also includes **revolutions**.

Toe Loop

Skaters use the **toe-pick** on one blade to launch and land on the same back outside edge.

revolution—a single, complete turn

toe-pick—the jagged points at the front of the skate blade

11

SPINS AND SPIRALS

When skaters perform spins and spirals in their programs, they impress judges and the audience. Some examples of those moves include:

Layback Spin

A skater performs an upright spin with head and shoulders dropped and back arched.

Camel Spin

A skater performs a spin on one leg. The free leg is extended back with the knee higher than the hip.

Flying Spin

A skater performs a spin in which the entrance is a jump. There is no rotation on the ice before the takeoff.

Combination Spin

A skater performs a spin and changes feet or positions.

layback spin

Arabesque Spiral

A skater performs a spiral in which the free leg is extended behind the body above the hip level.

Catch-foot Spiral

A skater performs a spiral in which the free leg is held with one or both hands.

arabesque spiral

Nancy Kerrigan performs a Kerrigan spiral.

Kerrigan Spiral

A skater performs a spiral in which one hand supports the free leg in the air.

Fast Fact

The Kerrigan spiral was named for Nancy Kerrigan. She won the silver medal in figure skating at the 1994 Olympics.

13

Chapter 3

Planning a Program

When skaters perform programs, they choreograph their moves. They also set them to music. The program is their chance to show off their best skills. Judges look for jumps, spins, steps, and other **required elements**. Specific skills must be included depending on the level of competition. Senior-level singles skaters, for example, must include an Axel jump in their program. Skaters get to choose their own music and theme.

Fast Fact

The Axel jump is named after skater Axel Paulsen. He created it and performed it during an international competition in 1882.

Various jumps must be included in routines based on a skater's level.

There are two types of programs that skaters perform. They are the short program and long program, also called the free skate. The short program comes first. At the senior level, the short program is two minutes and 40 seconds, plus or minus 10 seconds. For women, the long program is four minutes, plus or minus 10 seconds. For men, it is four minutes and 30 seconds, give or take 10 seconds. Less than five minutes may not sound like a lot of ice time. But skaters need **stamina** and strength to perform their precise and powerful movements.

Carolina Kostner of Italy performs at the 2014 European Figure Skating Championship.

required element—a particular move in skating that has to be included in a competition or test routine

stamina—able to carry on doing an activity for a long time

MUSIC THAT MATCHES

Choosing music for a skating program isn't as simple as picking your favorite song. When you're skating to music, you want it to match your age and abilities.

Younger skaters should stay away from music with grown-up themes. You'll look more natural skating to music that reflects your personality and style. The music shouldn't overpower you on the ice. Instead, it should complement your skating skills.

Singles skating moves should reflect the mood of the music.

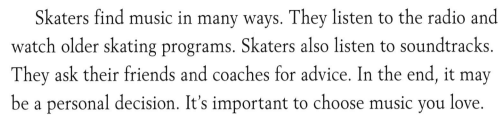

Making the Choice

Skaters find music in many ways. They listen to the radio and watch older skating programs. Skaters also listen to soundtracks. They ask their friends and coaches for advice. In the end, it may be a personal decision. It's important to choose music you love.

It takes a long time to perfect a program. That means you'll hear the music you choose over and over while you practice. You may use it for more than a year in competitions. The music also

determines the kind of program you get to perform. After all, the choreography needs to match the music. If you have a certain mood or style in mind for your performance, you need music that sets the tone.

Fast Fact

The ISU rules banned songs with words in competitive programs until 2014.

IMPRESS THE JUDGES

A competitive skater earns a technical score from judges. The ISU has set a level of difficulty and base value of points for each skating skill. A skater gains points for performing skills well and loses points for performing them poorly. The points on all of the skills in a program are totaled to come up with a skater's technical score.

A skater also earns a presentation score. Skaters need to show they have mastered **technique**. Judges look for clean movements when skaters perform steps and turns. They want to see that skaters can move in various directions and change their speed and power.

Mao Asada and her coach Nobuo Sato wait for her score.

That's not all skaters are scored on in their presentation score, however. Judges look at four other parts of a program as well.

technique—a method or a way of doing something that requires skill

Transitions

Programs link skating skills together. Judges base their scores on how well skaters can move from one element to another.

Performance

Skating competitively combines skating with music. Judges watch skaters for physical, intellectual, and emotional connections with the music they have chosen. Judges also look for ways skaters show what makes them different from others on the ice.

Composition

Skaters make choices about how their movements will be arranged to the music. Judges want to see that the arrangement has a purpose. It should convey an idea, concept, vision, or mood. For example, Canadian skater Brian Orser skated to "Jellicle Songs" at the 1988 Olympics. His playful movements matched the tone of the music.

Interpretation

Skaters also interpret the music. Judges are interested in how skaters express the music's character through their movements.

Chapter 4

Skating to Be the Best

Serious skaters perfect their moves to advance in the sport. They often skate four to six days each week. They practice **edge-work** and train to improve their speed and **agility**. Skaters also practice skills they plan to perform. Practice sessions generally last 45 minutes to 1 hour.

Lessons help beginners as well as more advanced skaters improve. Group lessons are great, but private lessons are even better. In a private lesson, one skater gets all of a coach's attention. Some serious figure skaters have private lessons daily.

Those who dream of skating in the U.S. National Championships, the World Championships, or the Olympics have to step it up even more. **Elite** skaters practice more than once a day, hitting the ice both before and after school. They spend 3 to 4 hours on the ice every day. They need an excellent coach to guide them along the way.

edge-work—using skate edges to practice and perform skills
agility—the ability to move in a quick and easy way
elite—a figure skater who has reached the highest level of competition

Fast Fact

By the time a figure skater reaches the Olympics, he or she has typically trained for 10 to 15 years.

Getting the Edge

Edge-work has to be practiced on the ice. Figure skaters drill by performing skills forward and backward and turning both left and right. They learn to use the inside and outside edges of each skate blade with control and grace. Inline skating can help with ankle control, but only on-ice training teaches skaters to use their blades.

OFF-ICE TRAINING

In addition to training on the ice, serious skaters train off the ice too. Many take ballet classes. They also do conditioning exercises to gain agility, power, strength, and balance. Each of these skills can help them on the ice. Agility exercises help figure skaters change direction quickly and easily. Power, strength, and core exercises build muscles so figure skaters can move with more force on the ice. Balance exercises help skaters maintain their center of gravity when balancing over their narrow skate blades.

Ballet can help you be a stronger, more graceful skater.

In addition to training on and off the ice, elite skaters take care of their bodies in other ways too. Nutrition is a major concern. Skaters get energy from healthy foods such as lean

proteins, fruits, and vegetables. They avoid junk foods, such as chips and sugary snacks. They also don't skimp on sleep. Proper rest gives them the energy to keep up with busy schedules and intense training.

Fast Fact

Jackson Haines, a Viennese ballet master, introduced ballet and dance elements into figure skating during the 1860s.

MENTAL FITNESS MATTERS

It's natural to feel nervous about competing. Some stress can be good. It gets skaters to practice and work hard in advance. On competition day, it makes the heart race. Stress triggers the release of adrenaline, which gives skaters energy. It also helps skaters focus their attention during the program.

Too much anxiety can become a problem, however. It can rob skaters of the joy they feel while practicing and performing. It can lead them to think negatively about their abilities. They may start to believe they'll fail. Negative thinking can even cause their fears to come true.

Elite skaters know how much mental fitness matters. They control their anxiety through techniques all skaters can use. They memorize their programs, so they don't have to worry which skill comes next. They practice their programs in their heads in real time. They imagine performing each skill perfectly. Sometimes, they even practice feeling anxiety and then feeling the anxiety disappear. Elite skaters also use physical techniques to relieve anxiety. They listen to their programs' music and walk through the programs instead of skating.

Fast Fact

U.S. national champion Gracie Gold calms down before competitions by juggling.

Gracie Gold

Chapter 5

Singles Skating Legends

OKSANA BAIUL

Oksana Baiul was born in Ukraine and started skating at age 4. By 7 she was competing — and winning. At age 13 she moved in with her skating coach. Her mother and grandparents had died. She wanted to keep skating, and she had nowhere else to go.

Oksana was 16 years old when she competed in the Olympics in 1994. She became the second youngest skater to win an Olympic gold medal. Afterward she moved to the United States. She toured as a professional skater. She also wrote two books, developed a clothing line, and appeared on television on reality shows and as an actress.

Oksana Baiul

SCOTT HAMILTON

American skater Scott Hamilton excelled as a figure skater even as a child with health problems. He had Shwachman syndrome, which made it difficult for his body to absorb nutrients. Still, at age 11 he was competing.

Skating can be an expensive sport, and Scott was forced to take time off as a teenager. A sponsorship helped him continue. He went on to win 15 championships in a row. He also placed in the 1980 Olympics and won a gold medal at the 1984 Olympics.

Scott overcame cancer twice as an adult and started the Scott Hamilton CARES Initiative in 1999. He helps raise awareness and funds for the fight against cancer.

YUZURU HANYU

Japanese skater Yuzuru Hanyu starting skating when he was 4 years old. By age 8 he was serious about the sport. Yuzuru became a world champion at the junior level and moved on to win medals at senior-level international competitions.

In 2014, at age 19, Yuzuru set a world record for his score at the Olympic Games. He won a gold medal and was recognized as the youngest winner in Olympic men's skating since 1948. He continued collecting medals and setting records at world championship events. Yuzuru became the first figure skater to land a quad loop in competition in 2016.

YUNA KIM

Yuna Kim of South Korea started skating at 6 years old. She won her first international competition when she was 12. At 17 she moved to Toronto for elite-level training.

Yuna won many competitions, including the World Championships. She set and broke world records. She won a gold medal at the Olympics in 2010. Yuna retired after winning a silver medal at the 2014 Olympics.

Yuna Kim

MICHELLE KWAN

American Michelle Kwan started skating at age 5 and won her first competition the next year. By age 13 she finished eighth in the 1994 World Championships. The same year, she went to the Olympics as an alternate.

In 1996 Michelle won another world title. She went on to win four more between 1998 and 2003. In the meantime, she took home a silver medal at the 1998 Olympics and a bronze medal at the 2002 Olympics. In 2006 an injury forced Michelle to give up skating.

Fast Fact

At the 1988 Olympics, competition between Canadian skater Brian Orser and American skater Brian Boitano was dubbed the "Battle of the Brians."

Tara Lipinski

TARA LIPINSKI

American skater Tara Lipinski always wanted to win an Olympic gold medal. She started skating when she was 6 years old. Three years later she won a gold medal in the National Championships.

At 14 years old, Tara was the youngest world champion in figure skating. At age 15 she was the youngest female figure skater to win a gold medal at the 1998 Olympics.

After the Olympics, Tara skated professionally. She later teamed up with skater Johnny Weir as a commentator. They reported on skating and fashion at major events.

EVGENI PLUSHENKO

Russian Evgeni Plushenko started skating when he was just 4 years old. He won his first competition at age 7. By the time he was 11 years old, he had left home to train and live with his skating coach. Soon Evgeni was competing internationally.

Evgeni has won three World Championships and several Olympic medals. He won silver medals at the 2002 and 2010 Olympics. He earned Olympic gold medals in 2006 and 2014. Since then, he has been involved in politics, starred as a television host, and performed in ice shows.

Glossary

adrenaline (uh-DREH-nuh-luhn)—a chemical the body produces when a person is excited

agility (uh-GI-luh-tee)—the ability to move in a quick and easy way

bracket (BRAK-it)—a shape like a parenthesis mark

choreography (kor-ee-OG-ruh-fee)—the arrangement of steps, movements, and required elements that make up a singles skating routine

composition (kuhm-pah-ZI-shuhn)—arrangement of movements in an ice dance routine, including how much of the ice is covered and how original it is

core (KOHR)—muscles that control the lower back and tummy

edge-work (EJ-werk)—using skate edges to practice and perform skills

elite (i-LEET)—a figure skater who has reached the highest level of competition

intellectual (in-tuh-LEK-choo-uhl)—what is going on in the mind

international (in-tur-NASH-uh-nuhl)—between or among the nations of the world

precise (pri-SYSS)—very accurate or exact

protein (PROH-teen)—a substance found in foods such as meat, milk, eggs, and beans that is an important part of the human diet

required element (ri-QWYRD EL-uh-muhnt)—a particular move in skating that has to be included in a competition or test routine

revolution (rev-uh-LOO-shuhn)—a single, complete turn

stamina (STAM-uh-nuh)—able to carry on doing an activity for a long time

technique (tek-NEEK)—a method or a way of doing something that requires skill

toe-pick (TOH-pik)—the jagged points at the front of the skate blade

transitions (tran-ZI-shuhnz)—steps and movements that link the required elements in a routine

Read More

Barnas, Jo-Ann. *Great Moments in Olympic Skating.* Great Moments in Olympic Sports. Minneapolis: SportsZone, 2015.

Labrecque, Ellen. *The Science of a Triple Axel.* Full-Speed Sports. Ann Arbor, Mich.: Cherry Lake Publishing, 2016.

Throp, Claire. *Figure Skating.* Winter Sports. Chicago: Raintree, 2014.

Internet Sites

Use FactHound to find Internet sites related to this book.

Visit *www.facthound.com*

Just type in 9781515781882 and go.

Index